WONDERS
OF THE
WORLD

igloobooks

igloobooks

Published in 2017
by Igloo Books Ltd
Cottage Farm
Sywell
NN6 0BJ
www.igloobooks.com

HUN001 0717
2 4 6 8 10 9 7 5 3 1
ISBN 978-1-78670-875-5

Designed by Charlie Wood-Penn
Edited by Bobby Newlyn-Jones

Cover image: Scott Wilson / Alamy Stock Photo

Printed and manufactured in China

CONTENTS

Man-made

Natural

INTRODUCTION

All across our world, we have sights described as 'wonders'; sights which stun, amaze or seize our curiosity. Since the original Seven Wonders - ancient monuments of classical beauty - described by historians and scholars of the 5th-3rd centuries BCE, the list has been revised and extended countless times.

Only one of the original Seven Wonders, the Great Pyramid of Giza, still exists. But, in the places of those lost are countless items of natural beauty, ancient monuments, feats of modern architecture and cases where human beings have worked with nature and the landscape to construct the extraordinary.

Some landmarks are shaped by our ever-changing world, some are reminders of lost civilisations and inhabitation, others are dedicated to religion. All are reminders of our wondrous, transforming world, our impact on it, our development as a species and our place on the planet we call home.

The Earth itself is a wonder, revolving at nearly 1,000 miles an hour, travelling around our nearest star at 67,000 miles per hour, for over four and a half billion years. Because of the gravitational pull and other forces this creates, it keeps its spherical shape, even when the surface is over 70% water. It is the only planet we know for sure which harbours and supports life, made up not only of us, trees and animals, but complete ecosystems, coral reefs, rainforests and more. It also exhibits wonders beyond biology, as so much is also determined by geology, to which we owe our canyons, waterfalls and other rock formations.

While it is almost impossible to include every conceivable wonder, this book encompasses the most famous and impressive our planet has to offer, including natural wonders, the 'New 7 Wonders' as decided in 2007 and the Great Pyramid of Giza in Egypt, the last remaining of the original Seven Wonders of the ancient world.

LOCATIONS

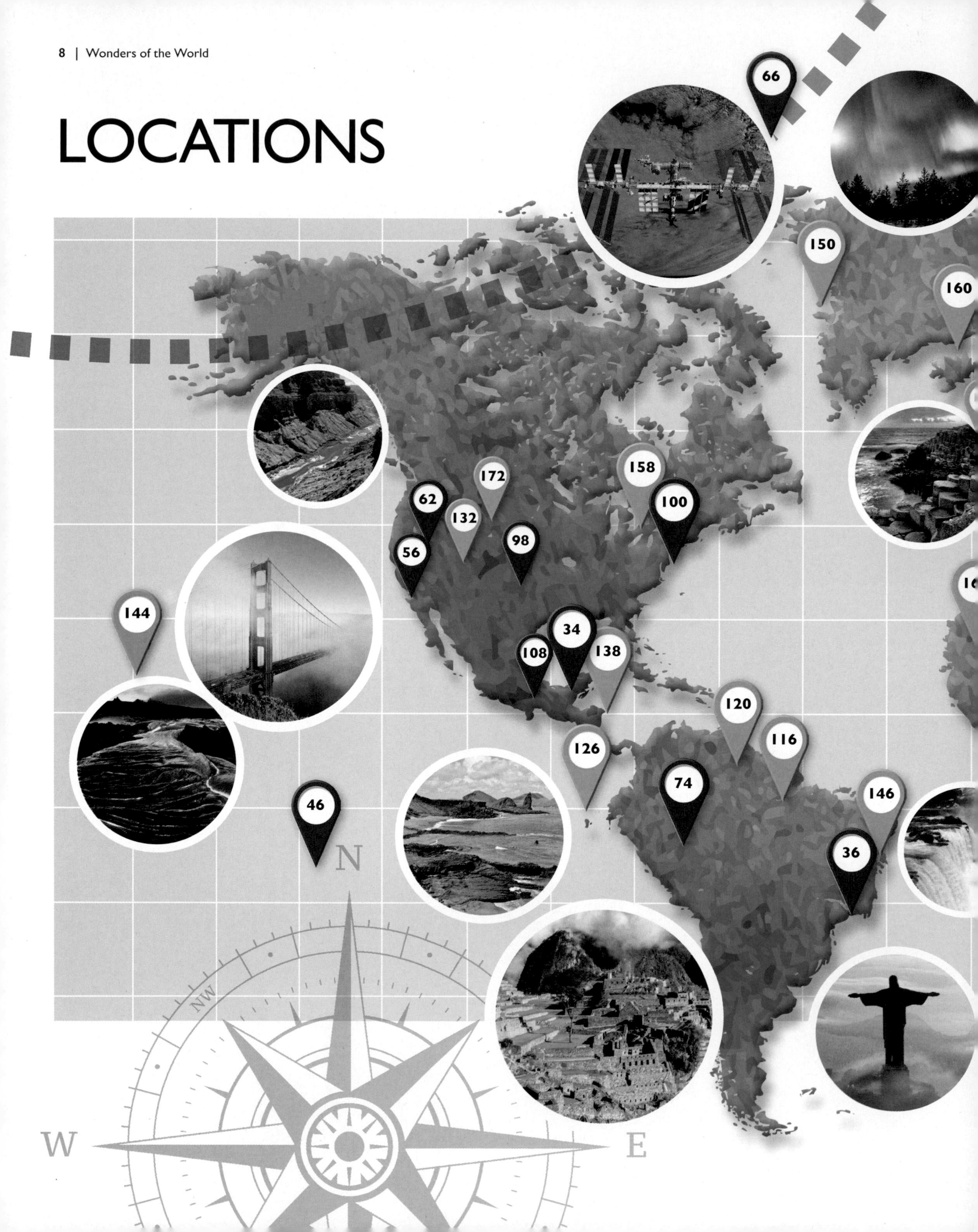

66

150

160

172

158

62

132

100

98

56

144

34

108

138

120

116

146

126

74

36

46

N

16

W

E

MAN-MADE WONDERS

The wonders we create are both vast and varied. They might originate from necessity, the desire to show wealth or power, or even to pay religious homage. We may use them to learn about our past, to look to our future, or to embrace the world around us. Wonders have added to the beauty of the world around us, such as Christ the Redeemer and Mont Saint-Michel, and even harnessed the powers of nature, such as the Hoover Dam.

It's amazing how long man-made structures can stand the test of time, revealing secrets of our ancestors through the level of detail, still visible after centuries of erosion, such as the toga-wearing Carytids of the Acropolis. Some wonders, such as the Colosseum and Carcassonne, are carried over as remnants from civilisations, while other historic wonders are those built for religious purposes, like the Sacred Mosque of Mecca and the Cologne Cathedral. Some – like Stone Henge – are lost to the mysteries of time and subject to speculation.

Of all the original Seven Wonders, only one still exists. The Great Pyramid in Giza is arguably the most famous to be featured in this book. Over 4,500 years old, the base is almost perfectly square with a difference between its longest and shortest sides of only a few centimetres. It is said that Pharaoh Khufu forced his own daughter into prostitution in order to pay for it.

Between 2000 and 2007, an initiative called 'New7Wonders of the World' was established to find new wonders from a selection of 200. More than 100 million votes were supposed to have been registered by internet and telephone polls. The final winners consisted of the Great Wall of China, Petra in Jordan, The Colosseum in Rome, Chichen Itza in Mexico, Peru's Machu Picchu, the Taj Mahal in India and Brazil's Christ the Redeemer, encompassing humanity's achievements spanning from 700 BCE. All of these - and many finalists, including Stonehenge in the UK, the Eiffel Tower in France and the Statue of Liberty in the US – feature in this book in stunning splendour.

In spite of all we have achieved, we continue to progress. In a world where technological advances and architectural wonders are becoming commonplace, it can also serve as a reminder of what more we might still imagine.

Although only a fraction of our tallest mountain, Dubai's Burj Khalifa is the tallest man-made structure to date, standing at 828 metres (2,716 feet), holding the world's highest observation deck on the 124th floor and swimming pool on the 76th floor.

Perhaps an underrated monument, meanwhile, sits proud on the skyline of Brussels. Originally built in 1958, the Atomium was only supposed to stand for six months. Nearly 60 years later, it still represents the ideas and ideals of the futuristic 1950s, not only a celebration of architecture and technology, but also of science and our continuing exploration and understanding of the universe.

Almost impossible to visit, the International Space Station, or ISS, floats 390 kilometres (240 miles) above the Earth and is the product of the cooperation of 16 nations. Building work began in 1998 and, in 2000, a module was added to provide quarters for the first three-man crew who would arrive later that year. It has been staffed continuously ever since, acquiring all manner of equipment to aid discovery and investigation of the wonders beyond our world.

What wonders does the future hold?

ACROPOLIS

Greece

Once a defensive stronghold, Acropolis translates as 'upper city' and the flat-topped rock rises 150 metres (490 feet) above modern Athens. There are other acropoleis, but none match 'The Acropolis' in terms of scale or quality of its structures, most of which date back to the 5th century BCE. The crowning glory is the Parthenon, a former temple to Athena, after whom the city is named. Its design utilises symmetry and subtle optical illusions and is fabulously sculpted.

ALHAMBRA PALACE

Spain

Dating back to the reign of the Muslim Moorish Emirs in Al-Andalusia, Spain, the Alhambra is a complex of buildings, rich in architectural and ornamental detail. Apparently simple from the outside, the interiors are incredibly elaborate, Islamic in origin yet unique to this Spanish outpost. Started in the 13th century, subsequent generations added buildings, using light and water to create Paradise on Earth. Details include delicate filigree work and the white marble Fountain of Lions.

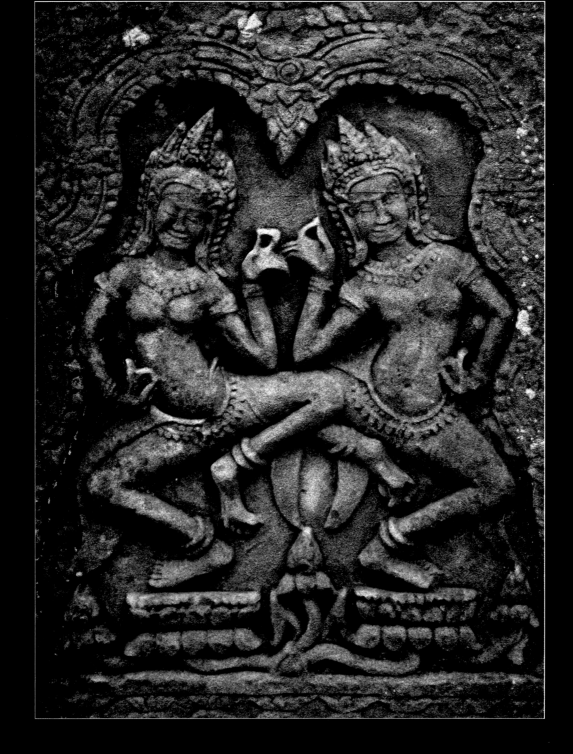

ANGKOR WAT

Cambodia

Made up of a wide moat, temple and enclosing wall, Angkor Wat in modern-day Cambodia was commissioned early in the 12th century. It was originally dedicated to the Hindu god, Vishnu, but later was dedicated to Buddhism and added to when the country converted in the late 13th century. The intricately detailed 820,000 square metre (203 acre) site has suffered neglect, resulting in a relationship with nature which is just as famous and beautiful as the structure itself.

ATOMIUM

Belgium

An architectural sculpture, the Atomium was built for the 1958 World's Fair and was only supposed to stand for six months, owing its preservation to public affections, excitement of the atomic age and enthusiasm for science and technology. Housing exhibitions, a restaurant and an observation space, the structure weighs 2,177 tonnes (2,400 tons) and stands at 102 metres (335 feet). Its futuristic shape is based on an elementary iron molecule with its nine atoms, magnified to a scale of 165 billion.

BOROBUDUR

Indonesia

Constructed in the 8th century, Borobudur is the largest Buddhist temple in the world with an area of 2,500 square metres (26,900 square feet) and constructed of over two million stone blocks. It originally boasted 504 Buddha statues, although now 300 are damaged and 43 are missing. The entire structure is built in the shape of a three-dimension mandala and thought to represent Buddhist teachings. It includes 3.2 kilometres (2 miles) of corridors and stairways relating to the journey to nirvana.

BURJ KHALIFA

Dubai

Officially opened in 2010, at 828 metres (2,716 feet) Dubai's Burj Khalifa is the tallest man-made structure in the world so far. Within, it holds records for the most floors (160), the world's highest observation deck (442 metres/1,450 feet high up, on the 124th floor) and the world's highest swimming pool (76th floor). The building includes a hexagonal core in order to withstand the earthquakes, storms and winds that Dubai is often subjected to, and can be seen from over 95 kilometres (60 miles) away.

CARCASSONE

France

With a history stretching back to pre-Roman times, Carcassonne is an exemplary preserved medieval fortified town and the largest in Europe. Contained within its turreted ramparts and protective walls are the citadel of the Chateau Comtal, a Gothic cathedral and winding streets that almost appear untouched after centuries. As seen today, the heaviest influences stem from the 11th century, but a fortress has been on-site for around 3,500 years and it has been a popular subject of film and literature.

CHICHEN ITZA

Mexico

The Mayan temple-city of Chichen Itza was announced as one of the New Seven Wonders of the World. Crowned by the 27.5 metre (90 foot) tall Temple of Kukulkan and including an observatory, ball court and sacrificial altar, the architecture dates back to around 600 AD, although the site was probably occupied for 8,000 years previously. The temple is perfectly aligned to the annual solstices and, with a stairway of 91 steps on each face and one final step, there is a step for each day of the year.

CHRIST THE REDEEMER

Brazil

One of the world's largest statues, Rio de Janeiro's Art Deco style Christ the Redeemer stands 39.6 metres (130 feet) tall and 30 metres (98 feet) wide atop the 710 metre (2,329 feet) peak of Corcovado mountain. Iconic to the city as the Statue of Liberty is to New York, it was designated as one of the New Seven Wonders of the World in 2007. Originally the idea of a Catholic priest in the 19th century, the idea started to become reality in 1921 and was completed and inaugurated in 1931.

COLOGNE CATHEDRAL Germany

One of Germany's most famous landmarks, Cologne Cathedral is famed for its Gothic architecture and being the resting place of some of the Roman Catholic Church's most important relics. Originally built to house the remains of the three Magi who were present at the birth of Christ, the cathedral's history dates back to 1164, although construction only started in 1248 and took 632 years to complete. Now, Cologne Cathedral welcomes an average 20,000 pilgrims a day.

COLOSSEUM

Italy

Despite its dilapidation, the Colosseum was the greatest amphitheatre ever built and is still an astonishing structure. Construction began around 70 AD and, when completed, the structure stood 189 metres (620 feet) long and 156 metres (511 feet) wide, with a capacity of up to 80,000 spectators. Also known as the Flavian Amphitheatre, it is a testament to Roman architecture and engineering with its exposed tunnels and cells. It became one of 2007's New Seven Wonders of the World.

DELPHI

Greece

Believed by the Greeks to be where the god Apollo, son of Zeus, spoke to the Delphic Oracle, the ancient temples and structures of Delphi date back to the 4th century BC and were built on the slopes of Mount Parnassus, overlooking scenic views. The most famous of the ruins is the sanctuary of Apollo, within which the priestess of the oracle, or Pythia, sat on a tripod, entering a prophetic trance as inhales the vapours from deep within the earth below her.

EASTER ISLAND

Pacific Ocean

Named by its native inhabitants as Rapa Nui, Easter Island is famous for its 887 gigantic moai, the defining stylized statues. The island itself is 24.6 kilometres (15.5 miles) long and 12.3 kilometres (7.6 miles) wide and is the peak of a volcano rising from the Pacific. It is the most isolated spot on Earth to have been inhabited and was once home to a thriving civilization of up to 10,000 people, which had dwindled to 2,000 by the time it was discovered by European explorers on Easter Sunday, 1722.

EIFFEL TOWER

France

Famous the world over as an international symbol of Paris, the Eiffel Tower was built in the late 19th century and, at 324 metres (1063 feet), was the world's tallest building for over 40 years. The iron structure grows by up to 18 centimetres (7 inches) on a hot day and the four-sided curved structure was designed to withstand high winds. Constructed for the 1889 Exposition Universelle World's Fair, building took just over two years. It is now one of the most visited structures in the world.

FORBIDDEN CITY China

China's truly splendid Forbidden City served as the residence of the imperial family and the seat of the Chinese government for almost 500 years. Began in 1406 AD and built over 15 years, covering a rectangular area of 72 hectares (178 acres), the complex of nearly a thousand buildings was supposed to represent paradise on Earth. Named because it was closed to citizens, it was guarded by a 7.9 metre (26 foot) high wall. Today, it is a vast museum and one of China's most visited sites.

GOLDEN GATE BRIDGE   US

The Golden Gate Bridge blends simple elegance with crucial necessity. Once the longest suspension bridge in the world, it spans where the mouth of San Francisco Bay meets the Pacific Ocean. Supported at a depth of up to 152 metres (500 feet) and a height of 230 metres (754 feet) to stand against immense winds and tides, the 2,042 metre (6,700 feet) long bridge was originally argued as impossible.

GREAT WALL OF CHINA   China

The longest wall ever built, the Great Wall of China began as several walls, built as early as the 7th century BC, to afford protection against raids and invasions. One of the New Seven Wonders of the World, it stretches over a distance of 8,852 kilometres (5,500 miles) across desert and mountains, interrupted by sections of trench, hills and rivers totalling 2,592.2 kilometres (1,610.7 miles). One of the country's leading tourist attractions, it attracts millions of visitors each year.

HOOVER DAM

US

Crossing the Colorado River on the border of Arizona and Nevada and weighing 6 million tonnes (6.6 million tons), the dam required devising specialist equipment and techniques during its construction between 1931 and 1936. This monumental hydroelectric dam creates and holds Lake Mead, which stretches back 180 kilometres (110 miles) behind the dam over an area of 63,900 hectares (157,900 acres). It continues to produce around 4 billion kilowatt-hours of power each year.

ICE HOTEL

Sweden

Lasting just a few months each year, Sweden's Ice Hotel is the only man-made wonder to feature in this book that cannot be visited all year. Every winter, architects, artists, builders and designers arrive at the small town of Jukkasjärvi to create a hotel out of 9,000 tonnes (10,000 tons) of ice and 27,000 tonnes (30,000 tons) of snow. The hotel includes its own ice bar with glasses made from ice, a wedding chapel, reception area and rooms for 100 guests. It shimmers under the Northern Lights.

INTERNATIONAL SPACE STATION

Impossible for most people to visit, the International Space Station (ISS) circles the Earth at a height of 390 kilometres (240 miles). At 73 metres by 108.5 metres (240 feet by 356 feet) it can be seen from Earth if you know when and where to look. The culmination of the work, expertise and resources of 16 nations following budget restraints and restriction, the construction began in 1998. In 2000, a module was added to provide quarters for the first three-man crew. It has been staffed continuously since and the crew are replaced every three to six months.

LA SAGRADA FAMILIA

Spain

Commissioned in 1882, the fantastical cathedral of La Sagrada Familia in Barcelona is not expected to be completed until 2026. One of the most ambitious building projects of modern times, the unique and impressive design is steeped in Christian symbolism. A façade on the eastern wall depicts the Nativity, while on the west is a portrayal of The Passion and 18 spindle-shaped towers represent the 12 apostles, the Virgin Mary, the four evangelists and Jesus Christ, represented by the tallest.

LEANING TOWER OF PISA   Italy

A renowned international icon, Pisa's leaning tower has become, simultaneously, an architectural masterpiece and a symbol of poor workmanship. Tilting at nearly 4 degrees to the southeast, it was built on inadequate foundations that were dug in unstable soil in 1173. Subsequent architects attempted to counteract the tilt over the next 200 years and a careful inspection will reveal that the 56.7 metre (186 foot) tower is actually slightly curved.

MACHU PICCHU

Peru

At a height of 2,430 metres (7,970 feet) above sea level, 'The Lost City of the Incas', Machu Picchu, hides in dense Peruvian rainforest between the two summits of Huayna Picchu and Machu Picchu, the city's namesake. Built around 1450 AD, the city is believed to have been wiped out by smallpox by 1572. Unlike other Incan temples and structures, much of Machu Picchu appears undamaged. It is Peru's most popular tourist site and, in 2007, became one of the New Seven Wonders of the World.

MECCA

Saudi Arabia

The most sacred site to all Muslims, the Sacred Mosque of Mecca in Saudi Arabia is the largest Mosque in the world and surrounds the Kaaba, the House of Allah (God), towards which all Muslims turn to pray. Also known as Al-Masjid al-Haram, the Haram and the Grand Mosque, it covers an area of almost 4,000 square kilometres (1,000 acres). It can contain four million Muslims during the Hajj, an annual pilgrimage that is a requirement of all able Muslims at some point during their lives.

METEORA MONASTERIES Greece

Devoted to peace, solitude and a life led apart from the rest of the world, the monasteries of Meteora perch on 60-million-year-old sandstone pillars at a height of 615 metres (2,000 feet). With a view over the Plains of Thessaly, near the Pindus mountains in central Greece, the first Meteora (meaning suspended in the air) monastery was founded in the 9th century. The first Christian monks there originally lived in caves and mountain crevices, meeting only on days of worship to pray together.

MONT SAINT-MICHEL

France

Mont Saint-Michel is a small granite island off the Normandy coast. Crowned with a Benedictine Abbey dedicated to archangel Michael, the island can be reached by sea or by a strip of land at low tide. Historically, it was a Roman stronghold, but buildings were added in the Norman-Gothic style during the 11th century. By the 15th century, it had become a wealthy pilgrim destination, but became a prison by the 19th century. It is now a popular tourist destination with a population of around 50.

PALM ISLANDS

Dubai

Started in 2001, the Palm Islands are entirely artificial, constructed in the waters of the Persian Gulf, off the coast of Dubai, to showcase a luxurious lifestyle, including opulent hotels, beach-side villas, marinas, spas, shopping malls and theme parks. The projects have stopped and started, with the most recent alteration in 2013 being the renaming and remodelling of 'Palm Deira' to 'Deira Island'. When completed, this island alone will have a surface area larger than New York's Manhattan Island.

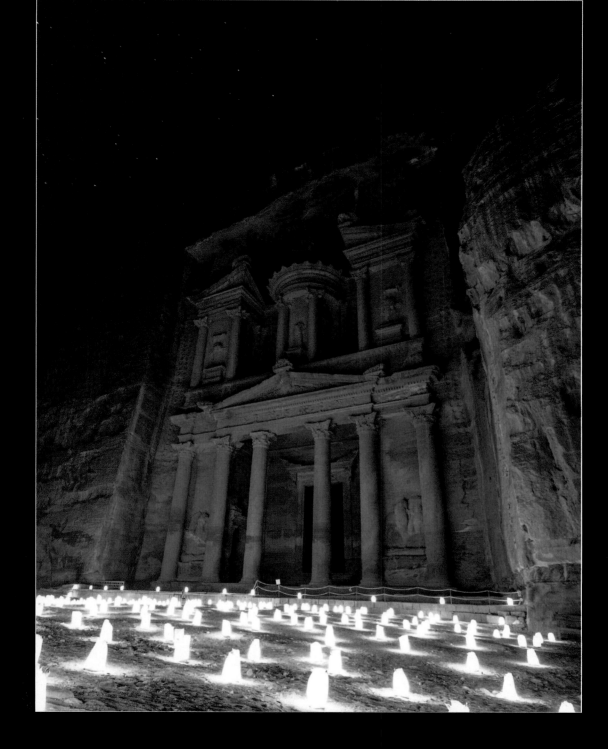

PETRA

Jordan

An intriguing archaeological site, the city of Petra is only reached by a narrow gorge. In antiquity, Petra was a major hub on trade routes and, over a period of 2,000 years, incorporated the architectural styles and traditions of its many visitors. Carved into the red rock of Jordan's Mount Hor are churches, tombs, monuments and sacrificial altars on a tremendous scale. Rediscovered in 1812, it has become a major tourist destination and one of the New Seven Wonders of the World.

PONT DU GARD

France

Dating back to the mid-1st century AD and remaining almost intact 20 centuries later, the Pont du Gard is a Roman aqueduct crossing the Gardon River and still bears the marks and graffiti left by its builders. Built on three levels, each supported by a row of arches, the highest stretches over 275 metres (900 feet) at a height of 49 metres (160 feet). Astonishingly, the entire bridge was built without mortar; masons crafted each stone to fit tightly and precisely alongside its neighbour.

POTALA PALACE
Tibet

The Potala Palace sits proud on Mount Potala in the city of Lhasa, Tibet. Home to the Dalai Lama until 1959 and dating back to 1645, the complex is 400 metres by 350 metres (1,300 feet by 1,150 feet) wide and 117 metres (384 feet) tall over 13 stories, with walls an average of 5 metres (16 feet) thick. Contained within are various buildings, over 1,000 rooms, 10,000 shrines and 200,000 statues, including jewelled and golden statues and the mummified remains of the fifth Dalai Lama.

PYRAMIDS OF GIZA

Egypt

Some of the most famous structures in the world, the complex of pyramids at Giza includes the Great Pyramid, the last remaining out of the original Seven Wonders of the Ancient World. It once stood at 146 metres (479 feet), but is now 137 metres (449 feet) due to the loss of the original polished limestone casing. The monuments form a necropolis, a city to honour the dead, including the three main pyramids, smaller pyramids and tombs, the Great Sphinx and temples.

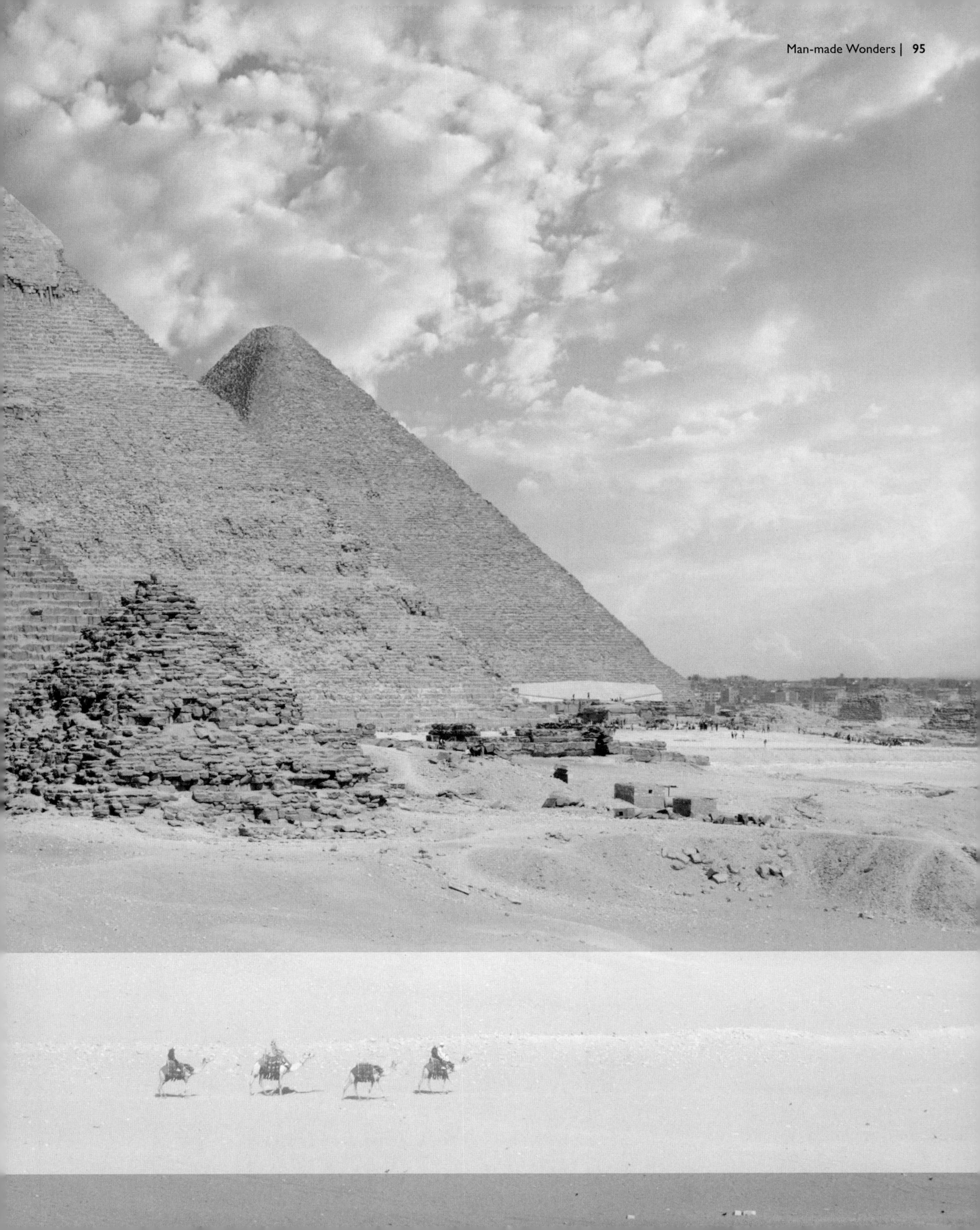

MOUNT RUSHMORE

US

Four of America's greatest presidents – George Washington, Thomas Jefferson, Theodore Roosevelt and Abraham Lincoln – gaze out from Mount Rushmore in South Dakota's Black Hills. Cut directly into granite cliffs, the sculptures stand at an optimum height of 18 metres (60 feet) tall and were created between the 1920s and late-1930s. Unknown to many, around 90% of the carving is actually done using explosives and the original intention was to sculpt each figure to the waist.

STATUE OF LIBERTY

US

Symbolic of hope around the world and an instantly recognisable icon of New York and the US, the Statue of Liberty – or 'Liberty Enlightening the World' – was once the first glimpse of America for newly-arriving migrants. The statue's height is 46 metres (151 feet), made from copper over a steel frame, towering a total of 93 metres (305 feet) above New York Harbor, standing prominently on Liberty Island, and was a gift to the American nation from the French people in the late 19th century.

TAJ MAHAL

India

Built by Emperor Shah Jahan as a memorial to his favourite wife and completed around 1653, the Taj Mahal is an example of an Indian 'golden age', merging Indian designs with Islamic and Persian forms. One of the New Seven Wonders of the World, construction took over 22 years, 22,000 labourers and 1,000 elephants. Despite undergoing some changes during British occupation and numerous wars, the Taj Mahal remains magnificent and opulent, attracting up to four million visitors each year.

TEOTIHUACAN

Mexico

While impossible to tell precisely who built it, it is clear that 1,000 years ago, Teotihuacan was one of the greatest cities on Earth and influential over other Mesoamerican cultures such as the Mayans and the Aztecs. Situated over 22 square kilometres (8.5 square miles) and home to up to 200,000 people of various cultures, the city stands as a testament to an extinct culture. It is now frequented by tourists and archaeologists, some of whom believe the city fell due to an uprising caused by famine.

TERRACOTTA ARMY

China

A surprise discovery as recent as the mid-1970s when farmers were drilling a well, the Terracotta Army consists of 8,000 uniquely detailed, life-size warriors lined up for battle, 130 chariots, 150 cavalry and an additional 520 horses, covering an overall area of 22,000 square metres (237,000 square feet). Created around 210 BC, the purpose of the Terracotta Army was to accompany Qin Shi Huang – the first emperor of a unified China – into the afterlife and conquer an empire in heaven.

VALLEY OF THE KINGS Egypt

Made up of buried tombs cut into a valley in the Theban Hills on the west bank of the Nile, the Valley of the Kings was the final resting place for pharaohs and powerful nobles of Egypt for 500 years. The most famous example is that of Tutankhamen, which lay pristine and undisturbed for over 3,000 years. Still not fully explored, 63 known tombs were dug into the cliffs and the Valley of the Kings has been a tourist attraction for hundreds of years, now welcoming thousands of visitors each day.

NATURAL WONDERS

Our world has certainly undergone some changes over the millions and millions of years since life began and the impacts on its landscape are not always our own. Much of what we see around us is a product of an incredibly long process, from oceans to mountains and the phenomena between and even beyond.

Based on its altitude, Mount Everest is our highest mountain at 8,848 metres – or 29,029 feet – above sea level, formed around 60 million years ago by the movement and collision of the Indian and Eurasian continents.

On the other hand, the Great Blue Hole of the Lighthouse Reef, near Belize, was formed during the last ice age when a limestone cave was flooded and later altered by what many believe was an earthquake. The largest known of its kind, the hole is 300 metres (or 984 feet) wide and 125 metres (410 feet) deep, but it is not the only one and larger may exist.

Between the heights of Mount Everest and the depths of the Great Blue Hole, Giant's Causeway defies imagination as a natural formation, while Angel Falls is the world's highest waterfall at an uninterrupted 807 metres (2,648 feet) and Niagara Falls sees over 168,000 cubic metres (6 million cubic feet) cascade over the rim of its basin every minute.

However, not all beauty can be measured in such a way. The sheer magnificence of the Northern Lights, which is still not fully understood, varies in terms of length, occurrence and even colour. Single monuments of nature have gained additional spiritual or religious importance, such as Uluru, or Ayer's Rock, in Australia.

Additionally, the scope of the Amazon Basin, a vast and precious ecosystem covering about a third of the continent of South America, really must be seen to be believed. 117 different species of tree have been counted in 1.3 square kilometres (half a square mile) alone and it remains largely unexplored. Any number of unidentified plants and animals, never before encountered, may still inhabit this region.

Truly, nature is a wonder all on its own.

AMAZON BASIN

South America

Covering 7,044,500 square kilometres (2,720,000 square miles), the Amazon River Basin is one of the world's most precious, fragile and mysterious ecosystems. In a single area of 1.3 square kilometres (half a square mile), 117 different species of tree have been counted. The region still remains largely unexplored and there may well be plant and animal species that remain undiscovered.

ANGEL FALLS

Venezuela

With an uninterrupted drop from the summit of the Auyantepui mountain in Venezuela of 807 metres (2,648 feet), Angel Falls is the world's highest waterfall. In fact, it is so high that much of its water turns to vapour before it reaches the ground and the mist can be felt up to a mile away. Located in the Canaima National Park in Bolívar State, this spectacular waterfall is well situated in a luscious landscape of picturesque cliffs and flourishing jungle.

DEAD SEA

Israel / Jordan / Palestine

Famous for its density and the surreal buoyancy this creates, the Dead Sea has a salinity level of 33.7%, making its waters around nine times as salty as the oceans. At 422 metres (1,385 feet) below sea level, the Dead Sea is the lowest point on the surface of the Earth and has a surface area of 810 square kilometres (312 square miles). Despite its waters being lethal to almost every form of aquatic life, hence its name, humans have believed its waters have healing powers for thousands of years.

MOUNT EVEREST

Himalayas

The peak of the Himalayas, Mount Everest reaches 8,848 metres (29,029 feet) above sea level. Home to two important monasteries, it is sacred to Tibetans and Nepalese Buddhists, who know it as Qomolangma Peak ('mother goddess of the earth') and Mount Sagarmatha ('goddess of the sky') respectively. First scaled by Edmund Hillary and Tenzing Norgay in 1953, it has been climbed over 4,000 times. It remains dangerous, however, being the final resting place of 150 mountaineers.

GALAPAGOS ISLANDS Pacific Ocean

Formed by six merging volcanoes only two or three million years ago and still in the process of formation, the islands lie on the Equator, 973 kilometres (605 miles) off the coast of Ecuador, over three tectonic plates. The 18 isolated islands are famous for their unique flora and fauna, including giant tortoises, and for prompting Charles Darwin to develop the theory of evolution, based on the apparent adaptation to the environment of 13 species, such as the Darwin finch.

GIANT'S CAUSEWAY
Ireland

A completely natural formation on the northeast Irish coast which is steeped in legend, the Giant's Causeway consists of 40,000 symmetrical and perfectly interlocking basalt columns, almost all of which are hexagonal or similar in shape. It was created around 60 million years ago when molten basalt lava erupted and formed a sheet over the area's chalk bed. The rock cooled rapidly, contracted and fractured into the crystallized hexagonal pattern which stands up to 12 metres (36 feet) high.

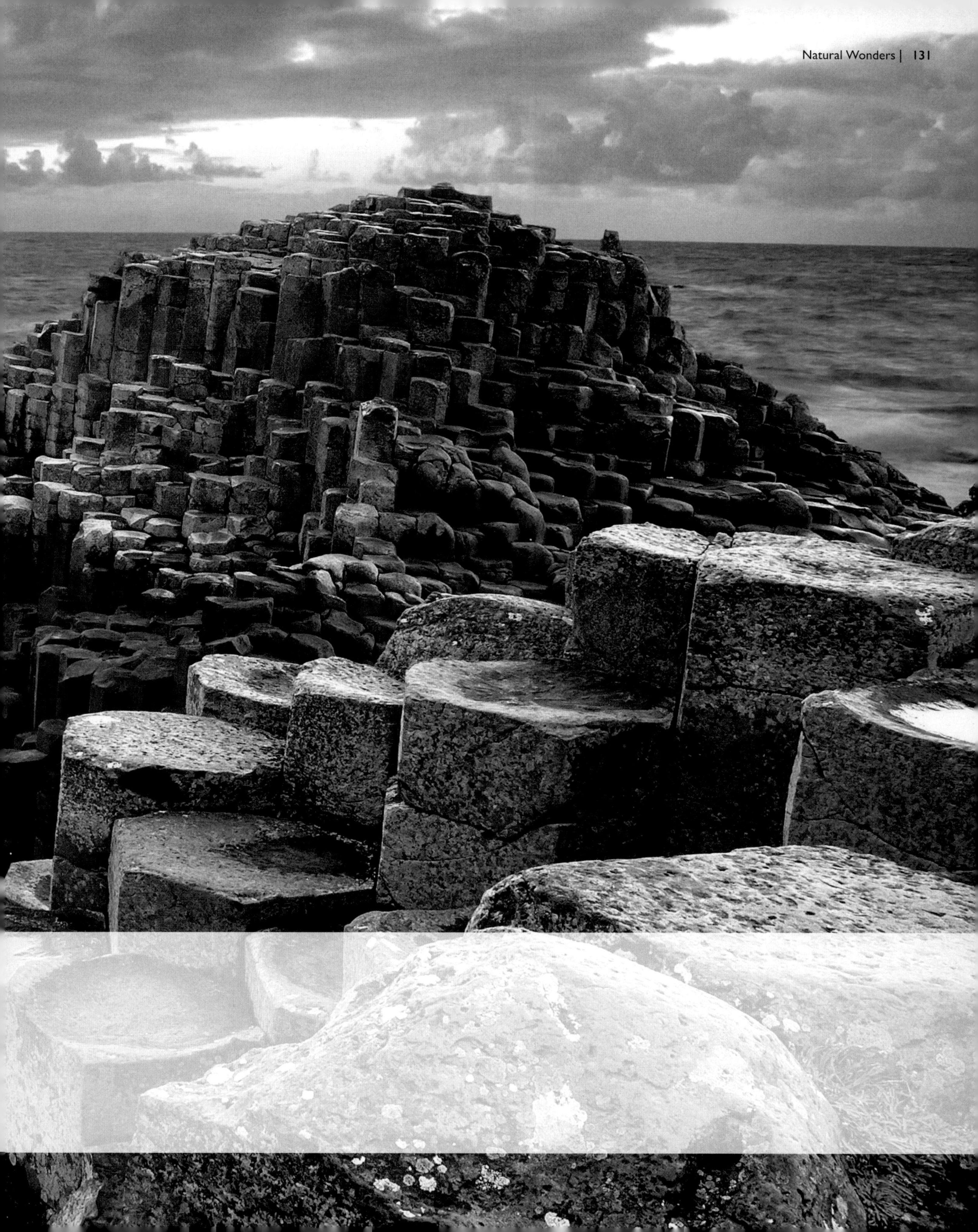

GRAND CANYON

US

Stretching over 445 kilometres (277 miles) from the Arizona/Utah border to Grand Wash Cliffs near Las Vegas, the Grand Canyon was formed over millions of years by the Colorado River. The width ranges from 400 metres (1,300 feet) to 29 kilometres (18 miles) apart and – in some areas – is 1.6 kilometres (1 mile) deep, revealing two billion years of geological processes. It has been inhabited for almost 12,000 years and is a protected UNESCO site.

GREAT BARRIER REEF
Australia

Made up of billions of tiny coral polyps and around 3,000 separate coral reefs covering approximately 334,400 square kilometres (133,000 square miles), the Great Barrier Reef extends along the coast of Queensland, northeast Australia, for 2,600 kilometres (1,600 miles). Effectively it is a giant, albeit delicate, living organism, which started to form around 20,000 years ago. It is home to 1,500 species of fish alone, amongst other species, including sharks, whales and birds.

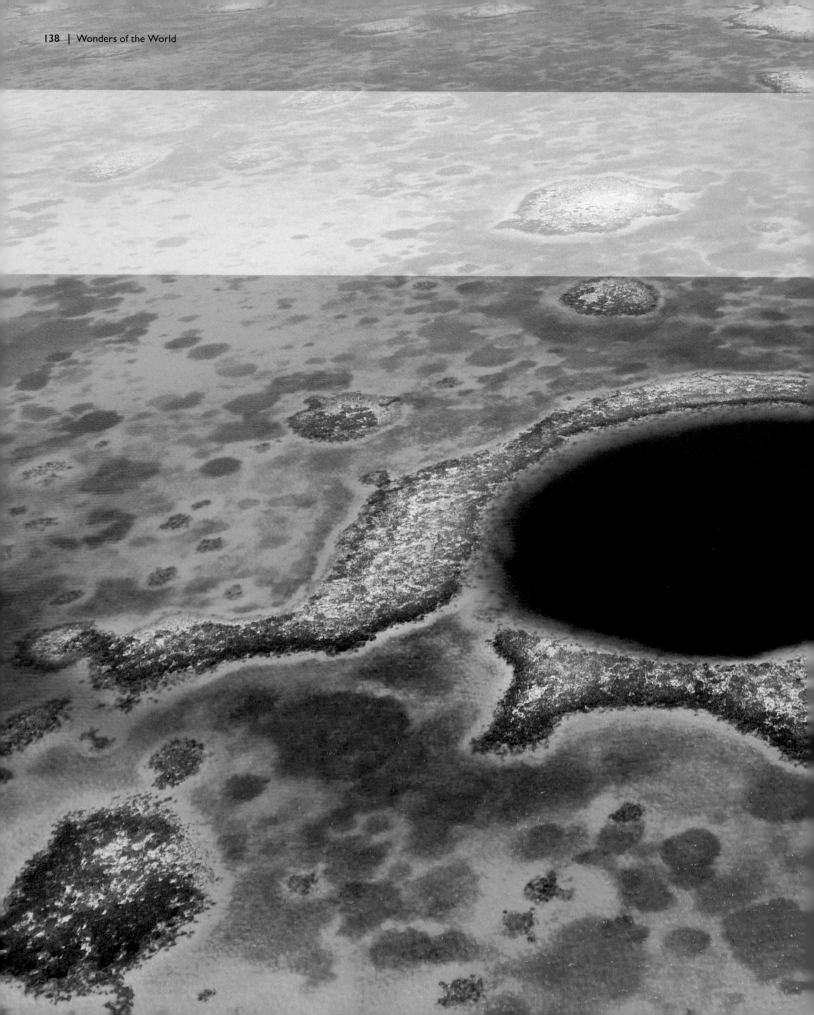

GREAT BLUE HOLE

Belize

At 300 metres (984 feet) wide and 125 metres (410 feet) deep, the Great Blue Hole is thought to be the largest underwater sinkhole in the world. Lying in the centre of the Lighthouse Reef, about 100 kilometres (62 miles) off the coast of Belize, its origination follows the end of the last ice age, when rising waters flooded a limestone cave above water and the roof fell in, possibly during the same earthquake which caused the entire cave to tilt.

HA LONG BAY

Vietnam

Made up of thousands of tall islands reaching out of blue waters in the Gulf of Tonkin, on the northeast coast of Vietnam, Ha Long Bay's name translates as 'Bay of the Descending Dragons'. Evidence suggests that the region was settled around 20,000 years ago. It covers an area of roughly 1,500 square kilometres (579 square miles) and the islands are formed from limestone and schist, eroded into columns by the sea which have also helped to form its many fantastical grottoes.

HAWAIIAN VOLCANOES

Hawaii

The Hawaii Volcanoes National Park covers an area of 1,309 square kilometres (505 squares miles) from Mauna Loa – the world's largest volcano at 4,169 metres (13,677 feet) – to the volcanic coastline where streams of lava burn and flow into the ocean. In between them lies Kilauea, in its constant state of eruption and seven distinct ecological zones including sea cost, woodland and rainforest where giant ferns grow and the K'au Desert of volcanic ash and gravel.

IGUAZU FALLS

Brazil

Made up of 125 individual falls, the Iguazu Falls is one of the grandest waterfall systems in the world – the most famous of which is the 'Devil's Throat', a horseshoe-shaped fall 150 metres (500 feet) across. The falls stretch for 2.7 kilometres (1.67 miles) across the Iguazu River and an average 1,746 cubic metres (61,659 cubic feet) of water spills over its rim per second, falling as far as 82 metres (269 feet) and flowing through immaculate jungle on the border of Argentina and Brazil.

ILULISSAT ICEFJORD Greenland

The Ilulissat Icefjord lies on Greenland's west coast, covering an area of 402 square kilometres (155 square miles). At its head lies a huge, fast-moving river that drops enormous chunks of ice from its leading edge which then float peacefully out to sea. The stream of icebergs is created by the gigantic Sermeq Kujalleq glacier, which often reaches speeds of 40 metres (131 feet) per day, depositing approximately 18 billion tonnes (20 billion tons) of ice into the fjord every year.

GUILIN KARST

China

The story book setting of the Karst Formations is made up of craggy, densely vegetated, limestone peaks and caves, scattered across flat plains, creating a magical landscape around the Chinese city of Guilin. Covering an area of over 5,180 square kilometres (2,000 square miles) in the south of China, the angular rock formations are a product of karstification, a process where soluble bedrock is dissolved by mildly acidic water over millions of years to create strange formations and cave systems.

KILIMANJIRO

Tanzania

Located in its own National Park, Mount Kilimanjaro lies northeast of Tanzania, close to the Kenyan border. The mountain began forming around a million years ago from volcanic activity and has three volcanic cone peaks, albeit dormant. Kilimanjaro is Africa's highest mountain and the world's highest freestanding peak at 5,895 metres (19,340 feet) and its snow-capped summit stands in sharp contrast to the immense heat of the savannah.

NGORONGORO CRATER Tanzania

Once home to early ancestors of the human race, Tanzania's Ngorongoro Crater was formed by volcanic activity
2.5 million years ago; the area is still active today. The conservation area covers 260 square kilometres (100 square miles)
and is surrounded by an unbroken rim rising up to 610 metres (2,000 feet). Mostly grassland with two small forested areas
and seasonal salt lake, the crater is a natural wildlife enclosure and home to 25,000 animals including lions and flamingoes.

NIAGARA FALLS

Canada / US

The mighty Niagara Falls consists of three sections – Horseshoe Falls, American Falls and Bridal Veil – spanning across the border between Canada and the United States. At its highest flow, over 168,000 cubic metres (6 million cubic feet) of water spill over the rim into the basin each minute. Combined with great clouds of mist and the constant roar created, Niagara Falls, the 10,000-year-old natural spectacle is one of the most visited natural sites in the world.

NORTHERN LIGHTS

Also known as the aurora borealis, the Northern Lights have been the subject of myth and still continue to mystify and intrigue.
Seen only in the highest latitudes, most commonly within the Arctic Circle, the natural phenomenon spreads dancing ribbons
of green, blue, purple and red across the night sky. The lights occur about 80 kilometres (50 miles) or more above the Earth's

SAHARA DESERT

North Africa

Covering an area almost as large as the United States, the Sahara measures over 9 million square kilometres (almost 3.5 million square miles) and covers most of Northern Africa. Over a history of almost three million years, the landscape has changed constantly; during the last 100,000 years, the climate has swung between drenched and dry and back and only 10,000 years ago, the Sahara was much larger. Its ocean of dunes and endless sands provides a landscape like no other.

ULURU (AYERS ROCK) Australia

Rising up to 348 metres (1,141 feet) with a circumference of 9.4 kilometres (5.8 miles) in the vast flatlands of Australia's Northern Territory desert, Uluru is a bulk of sandstone that seems to glow as it reflects the sunset. It is an 'inselberg', a sandstone plate that was tipped by geological forces and eroded. Like an iceberg, much of the rock lies underground. The site is sacred to the Aboriginal people and evidence of the Anangu people's beliefs can be seen in the ancient paintings.

VICTORIA FALLS   Zambia / Zimbabwe

Tumbling the waters of the Zambezi river 108 metres (354 feet), across 1,708 metres (5,604 feet), into a chasm cause by a fracture in the basalt rock, Victoria Falls is famed for having the longest unbroken curtain of water. This creates a constant roar and a cloud of vapour up to 400 metres (1,312 feet) high, visible from a distance of 50 kilometres (31 miles). During a full moon, it also produces an unexpected rainbow, also known as a white rainbow or 'moonbow', another natural wonder in itself.

YELLOWSTONE

North America

The United States' first national park, Yellowstone is a unique American wilderness, complete with natural beauty, flora, fauna and geothermal including geysers such as Old Faithful and Steamboat Geyser. It is located across Wyoming, Montana and Idaho, measuring 101 kilometres (63 miles) from north to south and 87 kilometres (54 miles) from west to east, containing rivers and streams, nearly 300 waterfalls, 1,700 different species of plant and some of the US' most endangered species.

PICTURE CREDITS